Opposites

written by Pam Holden

1

This is hot.

But this is cold.

This is big.

But this is little.

This is up.

But this is down.

This is fast.

But this is slow.

This is old.

But this is new.

This is happy.

But this is sad.

This is dry.

But this is wet.

This is wet, too!

This	but
is	down
But	up
big	little

point
and
say

Photocopy this page for flashcards

Emergent Level
Non-Fiction Set A

GUID READI		
A-B	1-2	1-2

DBZ550556

Red Rocket Readers

Engineered by
Flying Start Books

www.redrocketreaders.com

ISBN 978-1-877419-93-5

9 781877 419935